Weathering *the* Storm

Gael Lindenfield

Weathering *the* Storm

How to Build Confidence & Self-Esteem in the Face of Adversity

TRIGGER
he mental health & wellbeing publishe

To Stuart, my husband, whose unfailing support and consistently positive outlook underpins my own morale and has helped me through so many difficult times.

First published in Great Britain 2020 by Trigger

Trigger is a trading style of Shaw Callaghan Ltd & Shaw Callaghan 23 USA, INC.
The Foundation Centre
Navigation House, 48 Millgate, Newark
Nottinghamshire NG24 4TS UK
www.triggerpublishing.com

Text Copyright © 2020 Gael Lindenfield

British Library Cataloguing in Publication Data
A CIP catalogue record for this book is available upon request
from the British Library

ISBN: 9781789561784

This book is also available in the following e-Book formats:
ePUB: 9781789562019

Cover design by Georgie Hewitt
Typeset by Georgie Hewitt

Printed and bound in Great Britain by CPI Group (UK) Ltd, Croydon CR0 4YY

Paper from responsible sources

CONTENTS

· · · · · · · · · · · · · · · · · ·

INTRODUCTION

I am writing this at what is, for many of us, collectively, the most challenging time that we will experience in our lifetimes. The world is currently in lockdown due to the COVID-19 pandemic and people across the globe are at home, isolated from their loved ones and uncertain about what the future holds in terms of their health, career, finances and relationships. This situation has brought many of the issues covered in this book into sharp focus. For some, stuck at home with no connection to the outside world, this is a time of great loneliness and isolation, where reaching out and making connection seems impossible. For others, being trapped in close proximity with spouses, partners, family members or housemates, has its own challenges, with the usual irks and gratings of co-habitation being magnified ten-fold by the inability to escape and reclaim headspace. Many others are struggling financially, having lost their jobs or having had business opportunities go by the wayside. Others still are sick with worry about their loved ones, who they can no longer visit and care for at risk of spreading the disease. The list goes on.

The bulk of this book was written before the spread of the pandemic, and though in a few short weeks the world has changed to a remarkable degree, the messages and lessons you will find within these pages are more relevant than ever. When planning this book, I wanted to create an easily digestible manual of tips and tools aimed at specifically addressing low morale during tough times. It seemed to me that when tackling these issues, the negative influences that sap at our confidence and sense of self-worth can be split into two distinct halves: internal and external. With that in mind, this book has two parts; part one looks at our inner life and covers everything from mastering the negative voices in our heads to understanding our deep emotional triggers so that we can recognise and avoid issues before they arise. The second half of the book looks at our outer life and the external influences that can chip away at us on a daily basis. This section covers everything from our immediate environment and how it can be changed to positively impact on our mood to the food that we eat, our relationships both personal and professional, overcoming financial worries and harnessing our creativity as an outlet for stress and negativity.

With any luck, by the time that this book comes out the world will be a more positive place and we will have learned from this troubling time. Whatever the situation, my deepest hope is that this book will help you see through to clearer skies ahead and that the information contained within these pages will help you weather the storm and let the sunshine in once more.

PART ONE: INNER LIFE

1:1

GETTING TO KNOW YOURSELF

In times of great stress, the cacophony of voices and opinions can seem deafening, and it can be hard to take stock of your own thoughts and feelings against this onslaught. At times like these you need to step back, take a deep breath and focus on your voice inside your head before you are able to take anyone else's opinions on board. Being aware of your own feelings will also allow you to recognise potential triggers and quell rising emotions before they escalate into a crescendo. The exercises in this chapter will help you find your inner voice and give your feelings space to form before taking those of others on board.

PLAY TO YOUR STRENGTHS

"When I dare to be powerful, to use my strength in the service of my vision, then it becomes less and less important whether I am afraid."

Audre Lorde, poet

We all have our own unique package of personal strengths, and one of the big secrets of confident people is that they know precisely what is in their package and how to use each strength to advantage in any given situation. In contrast, people who lack confidence are super-aware of their weaknesses and spend most of their energy on either attempting to improve these or hide them.

Your self-confidence has probably been rocked by whatever problem you have right now. You need to give it some boosts. This exercise will help by reminding you how you can use your strengths to help you in this situation. If you struggle to come up with enough examples of your strengths, seek help from a good friend immediately. It is crucial to confidence to be able to keep your best inner resources at the forefront of your mind.

List three to six of your personal strengths in each of the categories listed on the following two pages and beside each one note down how they could help get you through this difficult period. The examples will give you an idea of how to do this exercise, but remember that your strengths may be very different (although no less useful).

My innate talents and aptitudes

Musical   Helps to relax or energise me; strengthen social contacts by giving free pleasure to others.

An accurate eye   Tennis – keeps me fit and releases tension; can make new contacts at club.

Creativity   Can draw my own Christmas card to save money; revamp the sitting room cheaply to boost my mood; use painting to relax me; drama to practise interview skills.

My core character strengths

Persistence   Can keep going even when I become bored or tired, so I could do a boring, fill-in job while waiting; I can fight through bureaucracy to check my full entitlement to help.

Sense of humour   Can cheer up others; keep my perspective; divert my attention from worry.

Optimism   Can spot opportunities; keep self and others motivated.

My special skills

IT   Opens research possibilities; can network more widely; work from home or anywhere in the world; on-line courses.

Selling   Can promote myself; apply for wider range of jobs; get best price for flat if we need to sell.

Listening   Can make new friends; elicit ideas from others; collaborate with others in the same boat.

Numeracy   Helps with redoing the budget; calculating real value of bargain; offering to be treasurer of resident's association and gain more power over decision-making.

Cooking   Diversion from problems; make interesting meals from cheap ingredients; sell homemade cakes/jams and sauces or use for presents; entertain possible good contacts.

Project management   View this problem as a project with a start point, milestones and finish point; keep organised and focused; review progress.

QUICK FIX:
Celebrate the uncelebrated

Few people celebrate their achievements adequately. Normally, only certain successes are routinely deemed worthy of celebration, such as passed exams, new jobs or winning competitions. However, in the field of personal development, these may not be the achievements that people consider to be their greatest. Here are some examples of what people have told me they regard as achievements – none of them was celebrated at the time, but they certainly deserve to be:

- Being a good parent

- Having a good relationship with your partner

- Keeping the peace with the in-laws

- Becoming fluent in a language

- Mastering the computer

- Going solo on holiday

- Getting over a divorce or separation

- Overcoming a fear of flying

- Growing roses in unfriendly soil

- Making a beautiful home

- Learning how to keep cool with the boss

- Becoming well organised instead of living in chaos

- Becoming a good manager or leader

This should prompt a belated celebration for some of your own achievements!

STOP STRESS
IN ITS TRACKS

"Tension is who you think you should be. Relaxation is who you are."

Chinese proverb

Everyone now knows that stress is bad news; the research findings about its threat to health and life expectancy are always making headlines. And from your own life experience, you'll also know that it depresses your mood, disturbs relationships and is an arch-enemy of progress. So why does it so often get the better of us, even during the good times?

Stress builds stealthily, and in its earliest stages produces sensations that feel great and often make you perform more effectively. The initial adrenalin rush is energising – it lifts your mood and makes you feel more confident (if not arrogant!). And after this, there is no stopping or turning back; you are deaf to any feedback and too excited or busy for introspection.

The secret to stopping stress before it spirals down to burnout is to be alert to the symptoms that indicate a descent has just begun. There are slight negative changes that can be sensed and observed which, at this stage, have few – if any – serious consequences. Once past this critical phase, however, most people have to sink to a point where hurtful damage has set in before they will consider taking action.

Of course, during difficult times, you are even more vulnerable to stress. So it will pay big dividends to carry out a regular spot check on yourself, which you can do very quickly, using the checklist opposite.

The following early symptoms are common ones, some of which you will almost surely have experienced, while others you may not – much depends on your health, age and personality. You can also add a few of your own symptoms if you have identified any that are not listed. Show this checklist to your partner and/or friends too; they may be able to spot the signs earlier than you will.

EARLY WARNING STRESS SIGNALS

Physical

- ❑ Tension headaches – especially those which persist when you are "at rest"

- ❑ Shallower breathing

- ❑ Less energy (perhaps taking the car or bus when it is easy to walk)

- ❑ Sweating more

- ❑ Unusual bowel movements

- ❑ Pins and needles when you stand or wake up

- ❑ Loss of libido (making the proverbial excuses)

- ❑ More frequent viruses

- ❑ Increase in allergic reactions

- ❑ Aching back or shoulders

- ❑ Restless legs and hands

- ❑ Cold hands and feet

- [ ] Increased PMT
- [ ] Congested sinuses

Emotional

- [ ] Increased anxiousness
- [ ] Moodiness for no apparent reason
- [ ] More pessimistic
- [ ] Not finding jokes so funny
- [ ] Persistent guilty thoughts
- [ ] Obsessive habits, such as wanting to check and recheck
- [ ] Feelings more easily hurt
- [ ] Apathy (saying, "I don't mind" more often)
- [ ] Mistrustfulness (wondering about ulterior motives)
- [ ] Cynicism (making sneering remarks; negatively generalising)
- [ ] Overexcitement (having a one-track mind about an idea; being dismissive of alternatives)
- [ ] Depersonalisation (feeling at a distance from the world around you)

Mind/behaviour

- ❏ Concentration wandering more

- ❏ Inattentiveness (switching off when others are talking)

- ❏ Reclusiveness (not joining others at lunch; partying is less appealing)

- ❏ Increased alcohol intake

- ❏ Increased smoking

- ❏ Outbursts of irritation (making gratuitous biting remarks)

- ❏ Less careful about appearance

- ❏ Indecisiveness (letting others decide for you)

- ❏ More cautious (saying, "I'm not sure" more often)

- ❏ Reluctance to delegate

- ❏ Making mountains out of molehills

- ❏ Going to bed later than usual

- ❏ Untidiness (being unable to find things)

- ❏ Disturbed sleep (restless; not refreshed after sleep)

- ❏ Change in attitude to money (more spendthrift or frugal for no "good" reason)

If you have ticked more than a couple of boxes, it's time to chill out a little. Don't just try to kid yourself that you can control the symptom/s – however good your intention, it is unlikely to last without making some lifestyle change. This book is filled with many ideas that are quick and easy to implement – so no excuses! Start experimenting now to find out which work best for you.

GO FOR "GOOD ENOUGH"

· · · · · · · · · · · · · · · · ·

"Striving for excellence motivates you; striving for perfection is demoralising."

· · · · · · · · · · · · ·

Harriet Braiker, psychologist and author

The chances are that if you are reading this book, you have a tendency to be a perfectionist. I am making this guess because the majority of my clients who struggle through tough times have had this characteristic.

To see if I've guessed right, look at the following statements and tick the boxes that could apply to you.

You tend to:

❑ set goals and standards for yourself that are so high that they become a strain on your time, energy or money and some of your relationships.

❏ find it hard to take a compliment without doubting the giver's sincerity or their ability as a true judge, or thinking or commenting on some aspect that could be improved.

❏ dwell on mistakes and failures for longer than most people and are not at ease when others try to comfort you.

❏ feel you could or should have done better, even though people are continually telling you that you have done well or you know your results are better than the average.

❏ believe that aiming for perfection is the key to success and should always be your goal.

❏ hate deadlines and wait until the very last minute to make decisions or hand in work so you have the option to make any last-minute changes.

❏ have packed schedules and less relaxation than most people.

❏ become irritated or angered by others who do things which are not up to your standards, even when it is not your responsibility to judge or supervise them.

❏ focus more on your own and others' weaknesses rather than strengths.

❏ have at least one self-improvement project on the go and more in the pipeline; if not, you feel guilty.

The higher your score out of ten, the more of a perfectionist you are. And if you are now questioning the validity of this simple assessment, you can add another three ticks to your score and read on! If your score was very low, however, I would urge you to read on in any case, as this will give you an idea of how to help others who have this trait.

And now the confession! I am a perfectionist myself and highly attracted to other perfectionists and perfect creations. So I have great empathy for you. But I also know that during tough times this is something that can render you more vulnerable to stress, being burnt out, pessimistic and feeling isolated and unsupported.

I am not going to suggest that you give up your perfectionism completely though! You need to simply tame it, especially in difficult times. The exercise overleaf will give you a checklist that you can refer to whenever necessary to ensure that you stay on a good-enough track most of the time. I assure you that doing this will free up considerable time, energy and possibly money. It will also make it much easier for you to collaborate with anyone who is helping you.

QUICK FIX:
View the big picture of your potential

Imagine that you are eighty years old. A large group of friends and ex-colleagues are throwing a party for you. Someone has been asked to write a speech about you, your achievements and why you have been and still are such an inspiration to others. What would fill your heart with pleasure and pride to hear in this speech? Use your imagination liberally to answer this question and make notes accordingly. Keep these notes somewhere you can see them (and perhaps add to them) regularly.

"People who are constantly looking at the whole picture have the best chance of succeeding in any endeavour."

John Maxwell, leadership and personal development guru

PERFECTIONISM EXERCISE

The aim of this exercise is to categorise your activities in relation to the standard you need to achieve. You will reserve "Gold star" standards in a few special areas of your life. The rest will be relegated to "Silver" and "Bronze". When you meet new circumstances you may need to do some rearranging. But always make sure that if you add something to your Gold list, you downgrade something else to Silver or Bronze.

On a piece of paper or suitable computer programme, draw three columns with the headings Gold, Silver and Bronze. Enter each activity into one of the three columns. Next, enter your main everyday tasks into one of the columns. Overleaf is an example of how I did this for some of my own activities.

"Always live up to your standards – by lowering them, if necessary."

....

Mignon McLaughlin, author of
The Second Neurotic's Notebook

GOLD	SILVER	BRONZE
Work	*Work*	*Work*
Writing books	Writing articles	Writing emails
Clients with a pressing problem	Interviews with journalists	Updating website
	Currently OK clients	Networking
	Talks	General office admin
Personal	*Personal*	*Personal*
Supporting my daughter	Health maintenance	House maintenance
Quality time with husband	Close friends	Other pastimes
Health crises	Reading novels	

GRADE YOUR FEELINGS

. . . .

If you are having an uncomfortable feeling, it can be helpful to give the degree of emotion you are experiencing a grade. To set a barometer, think of something that has, or could, trigger in you the greatest degree of the emotion that you are currently feeling. I've used sadness and fear as examples of potential emotions below, but you could tailor this exercise to any negative emotion that you are struggling with. Be it stress, worry, guilt or anger. Looking at the what you are currently struggling through against a worst case scenario will help give perspective to the feelings that you're currently experiencing.

You can use any scale that works for you, but I find the simplest way of doing this is on a scale of one to ten.

Sadness

10   Death of a partner or child

3   Loss of a potential job you'd hoped to get

Fear

10   Being on the front line in a war

1   Having an operation that is performed daily all over the world

This mini-strategy works because it makes you switch into analytical thinking mode, automatically reducing the degree of your feeling and helping you to feel more in control.

1:2

LOOKING AFTER NUMBER ONE

In recent years, mindfulness, or self-care, has become an industry, with people taking time out of their day to look in on themselves and make sure everything's ok – just as we would for a friend or family member who is going through a tough time. For some people, this act of looking inwards can feel indulgent or selfish, but it's important to remember that you can't look after anyone else unless you are also looking after yourself. Self-care can be anything from a daily meditation, to a walk or run in the park, to making sure that you're eating satisfying and nutritious food. The exercises in this section will help you find pockets of quiet in the noise of the everyday and give you the permission you need for a much-needed rest and reset.

USE MINDFULNESS TO QUELL STRONG EMOTION

Mindfulness is the name that has been given to a certain style of quick and easy meditation techniques. The essence of all of the different types that now exist is that you focus your mind on what is happening at present, either within you or around you.

DON'T GET TOO BOILING – A SIMPLE STRATEGY FOR DEFUSING IRRITATION

This strategy should be used as soon as you notice you are becoming irritated. It will send "switch-off" signals to the primitive emergency "fight/flight/freeze" response centre in your emotional brain. It can be done very rapidly and discreetly if you are with people.

DON'T	GET	TOO	BOILING
I	R	E	R
S	O	N	E
T	U	S	A
A	N	I	T
N	D	O	H
C		N	E
E			

Distance

Commonly, people grip or squeeze something when they are frustrated or angry; so let go of any tight physical contact. Take a step back or lean back in your chair, leave the room or "sleep on it" as Grandma might have advised!

Ground

If your anger response has gone into "fight" mode, you will probably now want to move around to get ready for action. You can steady yourself by putting both feet firmly uncrossed on the ground or lightly balancing yourself against an object or surface, such as a chair or wall. Then bring yourself back down to earth by switching your brain into thinking mode: try something like counting all the blue objects in the room, the number of circles you can see or counting backwards from fifty.

Tension

Release the tension out of your body by doing one or more muscle relaxers:

- **Clenching and unclenching your fists**

- **Screwing up your face and releasing muscles slowly**

- **Curling and uncurling toes**

- **Thumping or kicking a cushion**

- **Shaking your wrists**

Breathe

Do the following (or another) breathing exercise to ensure that your pulse is slowed down:

- **Take deep breaths in from the bottom of your stomach to the count of 3.**

- **Hold for a count of 2.**

- **Release your breath slowly to the count of 6.**

Neuroscientific research has shown that mindfulness meditations, such as the one I suggest below, actually do make noticeable changes in the brain's structure as well as in its activity. Findings suggest that there is a thickening in the tissue that processes emotion. But there is yet another benefit too, which is of interest to those of us who are approaching their senior years: the technique appears also to slow down the age-related thinning of the cortex area (where thinking is processed).

Try using the technique on the following page whenever you feel strong emotion rising. It can be done in a matter of minutes or even in a few seconds.

1. Close your eyes for just a few seconds and focus your mind's eye on visualising the physical happenings in your body. Imagine, for example, that you can see your heart pumping away, the blood circulating around your body, your lungs moving in and out.

2. After watching this imaginary movie of your organs at work, notice how your feeling sensations lessened when you diverted your attention to your internal physical experience.

Because this technique is so very easy to use, you can quickly switch into it in everyday frustrating situations. Here are some examples of when it could be useful:

*   You are driving and there is a hold-up that you know will last a long time.

*   You are in a queue in a shop on your lunch break from work and the person ahead of you has an item that has no price on it. The assistant has to ring the supervisor who appears to be on her break, so someone has to call the manager who is in the car park.

*   Your children are late for school. They are immersed in a quarrel about which one of them will take the only umbrella that can be found in the house. You know it will be good to let them sort the quarrel out between themselves

and take the consequences of being late. This will take a few moments, so you can sit tight and use mindfulness to control your escalating irritation.

If you happen to be an artist, you might be especially interested to know that this kind of exercise not only helps you to contain strong emotion, but also helps you to become more creative. Ellen J. Langer (professor of psychology and author of *On Becoming an Artist: Reinventing Yourself Through Creativity*) has studied the effects of mindfulness: "More than thirty years of research has shown that mindfulness is figuratively and literally enlivening. It's the way you feel when you're feeling passionate."

FLEE INTO BLISS
WITH A FLOAT

Just prior to my fiftieth birthday I had been going through
a particularly stressful few months, in the middle of which
I lost a very great friend who had become my mother figure
as well as my professional mentor.

I couldn't face a party celebration, so my husband took me
away for a de-stressing and uplifting weekend instead. The
condition was that every step of the weekend was under
his control. I had to just be guided by him through each
activity and would not have any idea of what I was going
to do next. When I am stressed I have a strong tendency to
become a control freak so, as you might imagine, this was a
very major challenge for both of us!

Very wisely, for my first activity he chose to take me to a
flotation centre. The result was that he was able to lead
me around through treat after treat for the next forty-eight
hours in a highly unusual state of consistent docility and
serenity. By the Sunday afternoon, I was beginning to think

I would never return to the real world again. But on Monday morning I woke up brimming with renewed energy and enthusiasm.

If you have ever taken a lilo on to a calm, warm sea or used float aids in a quiet swimming pool, you won't need convincing about its restorative effects. But now these have been scientifically proven to reduce the negative physiological effects of stress on the body.

A flotation centre contains small rooms with individual pools that are filled with water to which Dead Sea salts have been added. (These are renowned for increasing buoyancy.) The rooms are insulated from outside noise and also darkened. One research project in the United States revealed that when floating is done in such an environment, levels of cortisol (the stress hormone) are decreased by 21 per cent – an effect far greater than any you could achieve with similar rest on a lounger in a quiet dimly lit room.

Of course, you may not be lucky enough to have access to a flotation centre or a lilo on a warm sea right now. But you can simulate the "floating-in-air" sensation using meditative techniques. In my experience, these work best if you are lying in a warm bath that will help to relax your muscles; however, with a little practice, you can train yourself to achieve this "floating" state anywhere – even sitting on a crowded, noisy train. You may not reach quite the same degree of relaxation as you would if you were lying in a flotation tank, but if you feel any kind of floating sensation you will know that you are reversing some of the negative physiological effects that stress has on your body.

TAP YOUR TROUBLES AWAY WITH EFT
· · · · · · ·

Lorraine, a sixty-three-year-old widow, had always dreamed of having a comfortable and reliable car. When she received an unexpected windfall in a bequest from an uncle, she decided to treat herself. One of her neighbours who had been a friend for twenty-five years had a business selling just the kind of car she had in mind. She knew his business had suffered badly during a recent international economic crisis, and thought that she would do him a favour and buy the car through him. A good deal was very quickly done.

Sadly, a few months later, it emerged that the car had been stolen. The police became involved and confiscated it immediately. Lorraine was devastated. Her friend maintained that all the registration papers had been in order and that he'd had no idea that the car was stolen. But nevertheless Lorraine had to take legal proceedings against him in order to recover her money. She had no money to buy another car, and being a widow of senior age she could not secure a loan from any bank.

For health and geographical reasons, Lorraine was dependent on a car to get around. When she was advised that she might not get any money back for several years she was thrown into a deeply anxious state. Friends could not get her out of her house or stop her from repeatedly blaming herself for having been too naive and impulsive, and also obsessively worrying about the court case and how she would manage without a car.

Luckily, one of Lorraine's daughter's friends was a counsellor who had just done a course in a relatively new therapy called the Emotional Freedom Technique (EFT). She offered to help and persuaded Lorraine to try it out. Much to everyone's surprise, it worked. Lorraine's emotional equilibrium quickly returned, and although she still had her practical problems to solve, she was able to return to her normal active life. And, very importantly, the risk of her slipping further down into a serious agoraphobic or depressed state was avoided.

WHAT IS THE EMOTIONAL FREEDOM TECHNIQUE?

The Emotional Freedom Technique (EFT) is one of the new "power therapies", also known as "energy psychology", and uses the ancient Chinese meridian energy system. It is based on the premise that negative emotions are the result of a disruption in the body's energy system. In principle, it is similar to acupuncture but doesn't use needles. Instead, well-established energy meridian points on your body are stimulated by tapping them with your fingertips.

The process of tapping these meridians clears blockages by sending pulses of energy to rebalance the body's energy system. Shifting this natural energy changes the way in which the brain processes information about a particular issue, and tapping, while tuned in to the issue in question, is like rewiring the brain's conditioned negative response.

Sandra Nathan, a counsellor at the Hale Clinic in London who specialises in EFT gave me a simple technique you can try on your own. It can be used on an everyday basis to prevent worries and self-destructive self-talk from taking a hold on you.

EFT SELF-HELP TAP TECHNIQUE

Before starting, please note:

- **that you do not need to tap hard; you are just trying to create a gentle vibration on the meridian**

- **you must tap seven times on average at each point**

- **you can use either hand and either side of the body, but you will find greater success when using both hands and tapping on both sides of the body at the same time, where possible.**

Step 1

Think about the issue that's worrying you, then grade the intensity of the feeling (e.g. sadness, guilt, fear, etc.) that you are experiencing in relation to your specific issue on a simple scale of one to ten (where ten is the worst/ highest level).

Step 2

Tap on your karate chop point (1. the side opposite the thumb of either hand – see overleaf) while saying a positive reminder or affirmation such as: "Even though I have this feeling of (...), I completely and utterly love and accept myself."

Repeat this step three times.

Step 3

Repeat your feeling statement and reminder phrase while tapping on each of the following points:

2. Top of your head

3. Beginning of your eyebrow (nearest your nose)

4. Side of your eye on the bone

5. Under your eye on the bone

6. Under your nose

7. Between your bottom lip and chin

8. Collar bone

9. Under your arm (about 7.5cm below armpit)

10. About 7.5cm below your nipple

11. Wrist point (on your arm, 2.5cm from the wrist joint)

Repeat this sequence.

Step 4

Take a deep breath, stretch, and check the intensity level of your feeling again. It should have reduced considerably. If you want to chill out even further, you can continue to repeat the technique from Step 2 until the intensity level of your feeling reaches zero.

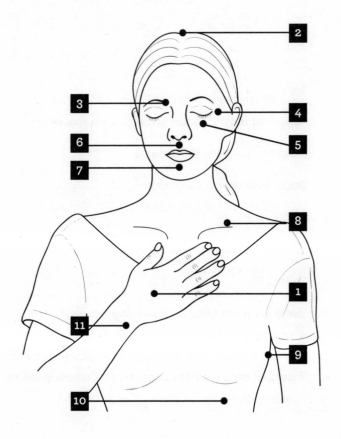

PRACTISE POSITIVE THINKING
. . . .

It's no news nowadays that positive thinking is good for you. Mountains of research have proved that it benefits your health, and makes successful outcomes more likely in work, personal relationships and sporting life. It has also proved (surprise, surprise!) that people with an optimistic outlook are more resilient to setbacks and tough experiences.

For some lucky people, thinking positively is an auto-response that their brain produces when faced with any challenge. They will always see that silver lining around the grey cloud and count on the sun shining in their favour once again.

But there are many people who automatically react in quite the opposite way. They only see the emptiness in the half-filled glass. In setback situations, they focus first and foremost on the potential problems and are blind to any opportunities.

Why is there such a marked difference? Some people are undoubtedly blessed by their genes and have naturally sunny dispositions. Others appear to emerge from the womb destined to become cry babies forever after. But subsequent life experience can also play a significant part.

We know now that, especially at an early age, the way we are nurtured and the role modelling to which we are exposed affects the emotional neural wiring. So those who immediately focus on the emptiness in the half-full glass have commonly had negative-thinking parents or teachers or repeatedly had disappointing or unhappy experiences in childhood. As a result, their brains needed to develop the auto-responses of anticipating the problems and fearing the worst as necessary survival strategies in preparation for fighting, fleeing or simply "shutting down".

Similarly, people who have been exposed to repeated or highly dramatic emotional trauma during their adult lives can also be hard-wired with these kinds of negative-thinking responses. Common examples would be soldiers returning from violent war zones or survivors of a major disaster in which many were killed and maimed. Even people who were previously naturally optimistic can emerge from these dreadful experiences with a complete personality change.

If your default thought mode tends to be negative, you should first reflect on what may be at the root of your problem. If you believe that it is caused just by bad luck of the draw from Mother Nature, then the simple positive-thinking strategy below should be sufficient to help you. If, however, your dark auto-outlook has been fed by some seriously negative life experiences, you may need to do some emotional healing before you can reprogramme yourself to think positively most of the time. To do this you could try healing yourself using my book *Emotional Confidence (Harper Collins, 2014)* as a guide or, of course, you could seek professional help from a counsellor or therapist. In the meantime, try the technique overleaf too. It should certainly start to help you, especially in everyday challenging situations.

THE GEE STRATEGY

This is a great technique for breaking out of a negative-thinking rut. When you (or anyone else) notices that you are thinking pessimistically, ask yourself the following three simple questions. Then try to rephrase your thoughts from a positive viewpoint.

1.   Am I Generalising from one or a few specific experiences?

     Original thought: "Everyone is too busy to help you nowadays."

     Rephrased thought: "Most people are willing to make time; Jane is an exception."

2.   Am I Exaggerating current problems, potential hazards or difficulties?

     Original thought: "This new restriction is going to cause chaos at the airport; I can just see us spending the night there."

     Rephrased thought: "This new restriction is going to mean longer queues until everyone gets used to it, so we must be prepared for some delays for the next month or so."

3. **Am I Excluding any positive aspects or potential?**

Original thought: "That woman's incapable of caring – she just thinks of number one full stop. I'm sure all she was concerned about was getting off the phone so she could get home on time. There's no point in ringing her again."

Rephrased thought: "Her response when I rang yesterday was certainly a bit abrupt. Let's hope I just caught her at a bad time... Perhaps if I try ringing her again in the morning and tell her that I didn't get a chance to explain the full story, she'll hear me out and have some suggestions."

AIM FOR QUALITY SLEEP

Peter and Rebecca's son Charlie is a sergeant in the British army. At a time when the war in Afghanistan had started to re-escalate and was dominating the headlines in all the media, Charlie was posted to the front line. Understandably, neither Peter nor Rebecca was sleeping well. Both were becoming so exhausted that their insomnia was affecting their work and also their relationship. They were irritable with each other and spending much less time having fun together. Neither would consider taking sleeping tablets; they wanted to remain alert through the night in case they received a call from the army.

Peter and Rebecca were right to be concerned and seek out advice. Research shows that sleep fragmentation and deprivation can have a negative effect on the brain for weeks. We have known for a long time how crucial sleep is for memory, but new findings have shown that it also affects the ability to adjust to change and find new solutions.

MAKE SLEEP SUBSTITUTES WORK FOR YOU

"A flock of sheep that leisurely pass by One after one; the sound of rain, and bees Murmuring; the fall of rivers, winds and seas, Smooth fields, white sheets of water, and pure sky – I've thought of all by turns, and still I lie Sleepless . . ."

William Wordsworth, poet

As I have suffered with periods of insomnia since early childhood, I have experimented with many sleep substitutes. Meditation is usually associated with achieving a spiritual "boost", but it is also now a proven way of achieving deep relaxation. It puts your body into a low-powered state and enables it to perform many of its vital recovery functions.

Many meditation techniques require training and a substantial period of time and privacy, but overleaf are two which are easy to learn, can be done in a short amount of time and are great as speedy re-energisers. They are particularly good for insomniacs or people who are chronically overtired. This is because there is less chance of falling asleep, as can often happen during longer meditations. They are also great for busy people because they can be done in public places. Perhaps my favourite way of using them, however, is during "waiting time"; they stop people like me from using up energy getting anxious (or even angry) over how wasteful it is. Try them:

- **during short train or plane journeys**

- **while standing in a very slow-moving or static queue**

- **when you are making a telephone call and know you will be on hold for a long while**

- **when you're waiting in the car, your office or home for latecomers.**

The secret is to do these meditations regularly throughout the day. This will avoid a build-up of tension.

THREE- TO FIVE-MINUTE SCENIC MEDITATION

1. Release the tension out of a few of your muscles by doing a few discreet stretches.

2. Close your eyes and recall in your mind a scene which conjures up for you a feeling of peace and wellbeing (a sunset on a favourite beach, a rose garden, a golf course or mountain path).

3. Visualise your scene in graphic detail. See its different colours and shapes. "Listen" to its sounds and smell its scents.

4. Notice and enjoy the sensations of peace and wellbeing that you should now be feeling in your body. Allow yourself to relax even more in this sensation.

5. Take a couple of slow deep breaths and open your eyes.

THREE- TO FIVE-MINUTE MANDALA MEDITATION

A mandala is a geometric design in which everything in the picture connects to a central point. There is an example of one on the following page, but an image search on the internet will bring up many other very beautiful and colourful ones. You could even draw or colour in your own. Keep it small enough that it fits easily into your handbag or pocket. You can then do this meditation almost anywhere.

Mandalas have been used for centuries all over the world to help induce a sense of inner peace.

This meditation uses the hypnotic power of their design to quickly induce relaxation of your mind and body.

Adopt a relaxed posture – uncross any folded limbs and give your shoulders a shrug or two. Put both feet on the ground in a comfortable position, slightly apart. Ensure that your back is straight and supported if you are sitting. Now follow the steps on the following page to complete the meditation.

1. Take a few deep, slow breaths.

2. Focus your attention for 3–5 minutes on the central point of your mandala. If your attention begins to wander, just gently bring it back to the central point. As you relax, your mind will start to "float" and your eyes will wander out to the sides of the design. When this happens gently refocus back again on the centre.

3. Bring yourself slowly back into the world by first squeezing your toes and fists, then taking a couple of slow breaths. Your mind should now feel clear and energetic. You may even have forgotten what you were worrying about. When you do remember, you may well have a new idea about how to solve the problem. This is because the mandala meditative process also stimulates the part of your brain that is home to your creative thinking "muscles". So this kind of meditation gives you two "pay-offs" for the price of one!

EAT COMPLEX FOODS AND BAN BRAIN FOGGERS

Avoid the simple carbohydrates which may give you instant cheer and energy, but will soon cloud your mind and depress your mood. You may well already know what they are, but here's a reminder of the worst offenders:

✗   Cakes

✗   Sweets

✗   Biscuits

✗   Soft drinks

Ensure your alertness by eating instead complex meals containing a balance of protein and vegetables or fruit and drinking lots of water. Also, keep a supply of alternative snacks prepared and at the ready. Fill a shelf of your fridge with the types of food that energise the thinking brain (you could also take a selection around with you in a small insulated box). Listed overleaf are some suggestions:

✓ Chunks of cooked lean chicken or turkey

✓ Chunks of cooked salmon, sardines, tuna or mackerel

✓ Shrimps or prawns

✓ Cubes of marinated organic tofu

✓ Hummus with carrot, pepper and raw broccoli sticks

✓ Walnuts and Brazil nuts with sunflower seeds

✓ Oatcakes or brown rice cakes

✓ Brown rice or pasta

✓ Low-fat cottage cheese with avocado slices dipped in lemon juice

✓ Lentil, aubergine and pepper salad with miso dressing

✓ Chickpea and broccoli and mushroom salad or stir-fry

✓ Spinach, asparagus and lettuce salad

✓ Blueberries/raspberries/orange segments/ blackberries/ kiwi fruit

✓ Low-fat yogurt to mix with any of the above fresh fruits

PART TWO: OUTER LIFE

2:1

ROUTINES AND REWARDS

Learning to recognise your achievements and rewarding yourself for your successes is a wonderful boost to self-esteem and clears the mist of self-doubt that can creep in at times of crisis. Building regular rewarding routines into your day is also a great way of injecting some much-needed positivity into your outlook and will give you a regular spark of joy to look forward to, no matter how bleak things may seem. The exercises in this section will help you identify the best ways to reward yourself and also banish the bad habits that are easy to fall back on when the clouds gather.

ESTABLISH REASSURING RITUALS

Do you remember how soothing rituals felt when you were a child? As a parent, I admit that I sometimes felt excruciatingly bored reading the same bedtime story, singing the same tunes and hearing the same jokes over and over again. But that was what my children demanded, and I soon learnt the advantages of giving in.

Rituals undoubtedly have a calming power. And it's not just harassed parents who find them useful. Religious leaders, for example, often use familiar ceremonies and songs to get their "audiences" into a calm (and therefore more receptive) frame of mind before giving important sermons or addresses.

Recently, while giving a talk at a business networking event, I mentioned something about the calming nature of rituals, and one of the executives there, Peter – a senior board member of a large company – shared his story with me:

Over a period of months Peter had had to be involved in high-level extremely confidential discussions with colleagues, lawyers and accountants about the company's dwindling profits and cutback plans. Unlike many of his fellow board members, Peter had been with the company for much of his career. He knew and admired the founder – a benevolent and caring employer who had often told the then novice manager Peter that, "Nurturing and retaining staff is the key to long-term success."

Outside the boardroom during these months Peter had to act as though nothing had or would change. Internally, he was going through emotional hell. He knew that just before Christmas the announcement of major job losses would be made and redundancy would follow very rapidly for many hundreds of excellent workers whom he knew had major financial and family responsibilities. Peter was on an emotional rollercoaster of sadness, anger, guilt and shame. He could not even share these feelings with his wife, as many of those in the firing line were also personal family friends and he did not want to burden her with guilt.

One morning, as Peter was showering, for no apparent reason he remembered an old ritual he used to start the day with before his work life had become so pressurised. He had taken a daily walk which he felt helped him to separate the two worlds of family and work. He would sidestep off the quickest route and go through a park and over the river bridge. While doing this, he listened to music through his headphones. Just before he reached the office he would treat himself to a cappuccino and fresh croissant in a small Italian café. While there, he enjoyed striking up conversations with many of the café's regular customers.

With this memory in mind, Peter restarted his "ritual". He claims that it helped him to "keep his head" through a very tough patch and that it continues to do so!

Researchers at Harvard medical school have found that rituals can even be used as a placebo to relieve pain. Maybe this is why my gentle exercise ritual each morning is so effective. If it is not preceded by my usual cup of jasmine tea in bed and then done to the accompaniment of a certain radio programme, my aching muscles never appear to get the same relief!

Try establishing one or two new rituals to help you cope. Choose ones that you enjoy and help you to feel relaxed as well. Overleaf are some simple examples that others say are helpful:

EXAMPLES OF EASY-TO-DO RITUALS

- Take 10 minutes at a certain time mid-morning to sit with a coffee and read the paper.

- Go out for a short walk alone after lunch each day.

- Listen to a favourite radio programme while having a bath.

- Get together with the family for a meal or snack at more or less the same time each day (one of my favourites).

- Take a break on return from work, shopping or taking the children to school to listen to or play music.

- Go to the cinema or watch a film or favourite show every Friday night.

- Meet up with friends in the same pub, bar or restaurant once a month.

You may already have your own similar kind of calming ritual activity. If so, stick fast with what you already know helps you, but do try to ensure that it doesn't get sidelined as can so often happen in the hurly-burly of difficult times.

Finally, remember that there is a difference between a routine that you want to do and one that has just become a purposeless boring habit. So the same series of actions can be a comforting ritual for one person and a morale knock-back for someone else – in the words of Dwight Currie, author of the bestselling book *How We Behave at the Feast: Reflections on Living in an Age of Plenty:* "One man's rut is another man's ritual."

QUICK FIX:
Top and tail each day with treats

The start and end of your day can often create a "downer" effect: this is when you are alone with your thoughts – when the stark reality of a problem or feelings of aloneness often loom largest. So it's easy to get into the habit of worrying the moment you wake up or when you switch off the light at night, especially if your day is so busy that you fall into bed too late at night, set the alarm for the latest time you can wake up, giving yourself a tense and rushed start to the day.

After one great de-stressing holiday, I realised that there was no reason why I could not do at home one of the things I'd enjoyed most on holiday – reading in bed. I just had to make waking and going to bed earlier a new ritual. I did that, and haven't looked back for eighteen years!

Choose one or more enjoyable activities that you can easily do and that will have the same effect.

SURPRISE YOURSELF WITH YOUR REWARDS FOR EFFORT

To maintain your momentum, it is very important to focus on rewarding your good efforts rather than waiting until success arrives. If you are having a very difficult time with a tough challenge, this is especially important. It may be a long time before you will feel truly satisfied that you have recovered or moved on.

If you've ever trained a dog, you'll know how important it is to vary the rewards you give them. This is why their treats are usually sold in variety packs. Every time you dip your hand into the pack neither you nor your dog knows what will be brought out. And while, of course, there may be some major differences between you and dogs, in this respect you are predictably the same! You can expect a much better performance from yourself if you randomly rotate your rewards. The surprise element is exciting, pleasurable and so much more satisfying.

It will pay you to prepare some rewards so that you can give them to yourself fairly quickly after you have made a good effort. Here are two suggestions:

- Buy yourself a number of small gifts, and wrap them in bubble wrap to disguise their shape before you cover them with paper. Keep these in a drawer or box, then close your eyes and take a dip into the pile whenever you deserve a treat.

- Take some plain cards and write out a treat on each one, such as:

  - dinner at a certain restaurant

  - a framed print or special book that you would like or a new accessory

  - an outing or weekend break

  - quality time with a certain person.

Pop these cards in a clear plastic envelope and keep it in your handbag or briefcase. Then, when you've had a success or taken a step forward in your recovery (however small), shuffle your cards, pick one out at random and give yourself that treat.

CHECK "COLD COMFORT" HABITS

Comforting treats must become a staple psychological food during difficult times. When you need emotional healing after a disappointment, injustice or setback, you should grant yourself an even larger helping. But be very careful not to choose the kind which I call "sting-in- the tail" treats – those which may feel instantly good, but which have a knock-on negative side effect. This is a very common habit among people whose mood is already depressed.

Rebecca was finding it very hard to move on after her relationship with her boyfriend had ended. One of the main reasons was that she could not face being hurt again. She had seen my book *Emotional Confidence*, and came to me for a few "booster" sessions.

As we explored her problem, it became obvious that the comfort stage was where she was going wrong. The only examples she could give me of ways with which she could comfort herself after a rejection were what she termed as "naughty foods", such as chocolates and coconut ice cream. As she had struggled for many years with weight issues, these were sting-in-the-tail treats that could never be truly comforting to her.

A sting-in-the-tail treat could have a detrimental effect on your health, affect your concentration at work the next day, diminish your struggling bank balance or irritate your partner. In the long term, therefore, they are likely to be counterproductive because they produce extra trouble and stress. Many are also guaranteed to make you feel guilty, just as Rebecca's did, and so will eat away at your self-esteem.

"THERE'S NO BETTER WAY TO ENERGISE YOUR BODY, MIND AND SPIRIT THAN BY TAKING CARE OF YOURSELF."

Stephanie Tourles, holistic beautician and author

LEARN TO IDENTIFY
THE STING IN THE TAIL

The table below gives some common examples to start you off on making your own "bad treats" warning list. It is a good idea to let anyone who might want to help you have some comfort look at your list too. You could also ask them to help you compile a list of good-for-you alternatives.

COMFORT TREAT	POSSIBLE STINGS IN THE TAIL
Drowning your sorrows	A hangover; saying or doing things you'll regret; liver damage
Sugar fixes	Weight gain; bad teeth; increased diabetes risk
Retail therapy	Unnecessary impulse buys; credit card debt
Cheap weekend break	Exhausting travel and sightseeing; bad food; dingy hotel
Expensive bouquets	Flowers die quickly; cost five times the price of a simple bunch of fresher flowers
Restaurant meal	Time-consuming; less nutritious; annoying music; overeating (usually); exorbitant wine

PLAN TO COMPENSATE YOURSELF

· ·

"If we will be quiet and ready enough, we shall find compensation in every disappointment".

· · · · · · · · · · · · ·

Henry David Thoreau, philosopher

Sean, a pilot in the Spanish air force, had a heart bypass at the age of forty-five. He was then placed on indefinite sick leave, although on recovery from the operation he felt as fit and able as he had been at thirty-nine. Many people might have welcomed this enforced retirement, but for Sean it was a blow which threw him and his relationship with his family whom he dearly loved into turmoil. He missed his work. The pressure had been high, but it had always been exciting. He also missed the camaraderie of his colleagues, his status and responsibility and the travel.

For Sean's family, the adjustment was hard too. They were not used to having him at home. He had three teenage children, all at different stages of testing the boundaries of parental patience. The setting of house rules and discipline had previously been the province of Sean's wife, together with her mother, who had effectively become the co-parent as she looked after the children much of the time. Both women now found Sean's intervention in their "zone of control" hard. The children (as is normal with teenagers) were quick to take advantage of the mismatch in the differing rules and degrees of willingness to part with money.

Sean could see no way out of this stressful situation. The family, including him, were too set in their ways to change much. He knew he needed more time out of the house, but another job was impossible as he would lose his sick pay. He had not built up a social life or any absorbing hobbies in his home town. His buddies were scattered across Spain and much of the world.

The friends of the family had inevitably been chosen by his wife and Sean felt on the outside of this closely knit group.

After a serious heart-to-heart talk, Sean and his wife agreed that he should go and stay with one of his close colleagues who happened to be on leave for a few weeks. This colleague was staying in a recently bought seaside apartment which happened to adjoin a golf course. Neither Sean nor his colleague had ever been interested in golf, but a neighbour invited them to join him at his club for a round. This was the start of a passion that probably saved Sean's marriage. It very quickly became apparent that Sean had innate golfing talents. With his friend's encouragement, he decided to treat himself to twenty lessons with a professional and membership of his local club on his return home. They agreed he deserved to spend this money on himself as compensation for having lost the working and social life that he had loved.

Compensating yourself for the emotional hurt you have suffered is an essential step in the psychological healing process. Very often, in difficult times you can be so involved in sorting out practical issues that your emotional-health needs are neglected. The only compensation that is likely to be given priority is the financial kind, if that is possible. But the type of compensation that I believe gives a truly satisfying emotional and morale lift is that which Sean gave himself. The golf idea worked because it fitted with the hurt that he had felt by being retired so early. It boosted his self-esteem, as it was using his best talents, gave him a friendship circle with men that he missed and gave him and his family the opportunity to get back to playing the roles that had worked so well for them all for many years.

WHAT KIND OF COMPENSATION MIGHT WORK FOR YOU?

The key to choosing well is to think of the deficit or deficits that your setback has left you with. These can be psychological, material, financial, social, personal growth or health issues. Very often, it is a mixed bag of a few of these. But for the purposes of compensation, selecting one key area may work well enough for emotional healing. Here are some examples to start you thinking:

Deficit: Loss of trust in a friendship
Compensation: Join a club to meet new friends

Deficit: Loss of optimistic outlook
Compensation: Books of encouraging quotes; Stream films or documentaries about inspirational people

Deficit: Physical ability
Compensation: Interest or hobby that develops mental strengths

Deficit: Loss of garden due to repossession of house
Compensation: A flat adjacent to a beautiful park that is maintained by someone else

2:2

SPARK
CREATIVITY

As children, our world is a riot of colourful creativity, from game playing and acting to singing, dancing, painting and drawing, but as we grow and the shackles of adulthood take priority, we lose these creative outputs and our confidence to undertake them. The exercises in this chapter are designed to help you recover some of that creative spark, allowing you to channel your emotions into creating something beautiful and opening the floodgates to let colour flow back into your life.

REVIVE A
HIDDEN
TALENT

· · · · · · · · · · · · · ·

*"Adversity has the effect of
eliciting talents which, in
prosperous circumstances
would have lain dormant."*

· · · · · · · · · · · · · ·

Horace, Roman poet and philosopher

Joyce, my Spanish teacher and friend, was diagnosed with
Parkinson's disease in her early forties. For the first couple
of months she was in a state of shock and very worried
about her future. But then her positive fighting nature
kicked back in again. She found out as much as she could
about the disease and learnt that she could ameliorate her
symptoms considerably if she exercised.

In her younger years she'd had a talent for crafts and
decided to start that hobby again. She now makes the most

beautiful cards and framed pictures using intricate paper "sculptures" and calligraphy, and gives them as presents to friends. This work has improved the mobility of her fingers and hands considerably. I have one of her pictures in my office by my computer, and it is a constant source of inspiration.

Do you have a talent for art or a hobby or sport that has fallen by the wayside – something that you could revive right now? If you can't think of one, perhaps you have another kind of talent that is underused, such as organising parties or speaking a language?

EXPERIMENT WITH ECCENTRICITY

"Nobody realises that some people expend tremendous energy merely trying to be normal."

Albert Camus, writer and philosopher

It can be very enlightening and energising to edge ourselves out of our character ruts from time to time. When life is going fine, we may do this purely for fun at Halloween or on a trip to Disneyland. But during tough times a push outside our comfortable character zone can be incredibly helpful.

Problem situations often require you to act and think in ways that are unusual for you. This exercise is one that I have used for many years with clients and it has proved to be a great confidence-builder for them, as well as giving insight into hidden or forgotten aspects of their personalities. Remember that it should be fun and that it won't do your self-esteem any good if you do something which offends others.

Here are a few examples to start you thinking.

Go "shopping" without money

Take a small amount of emergency cash with you, but no credit cards. You can then feel free to experiment with trying on clothes to your heart's content. I once tried this out and learnt from it. I was trying on a hat that I thought looked hilariously stupid on me. Yet I was told in all seriousness by a couple of shoppers that it suited me. This made me realise that I had become a bit too "reserved" in the way I dress. In my younger days, I had quite a reputation for wearing eye-catching clothes and had had fun wearing them.

Buy and wear an unusual accessory

Second-hand shops and stalls are a great place to find these cheaply. Buy them and wear them with panache at some event. One senior executive client wore a tie which had Rudolph the Reindeer's nose flashing red to the office party. This was very out of character for him and a positive surprise for those who thought they knew him well.

Order an unusual breakfast in a café

Another client of mine ordered an ice-cream dessert for breakfast in the middle of winter. As a result, he received some good-humoured teasing from the waiter and fellow eaters. This was great for him because he had slipped into becoming overly serious as a result of his difficulties. Lightening up didn't improve his bank balance, but it didn't diminish it either, and his wife appreciated the return of his sense of humour.

QUICK FIX:
Hum yourself happy

This is a great, simple tip from Dr Daniel G. Amen, author of *Change Your Brain, Change Your Life*. Dr Amen, a psychiatrist and neuroscientist (which means that his wisdom is based on seeing for himself how the brain reacts when people do certain things, as well as his considerable clinical experience), says that humming enhances both mood and memory.

So you can lift your spirits and tune your mind at the same time. Dr Amen suggests that we consciously focus on humming from time to time during the day. But don't wait until the going gets any tougher; give your morale and momentum an easy boost by starting a happy hum right now!

MAKE A MOOD
MUSIC COMPILATION

Music has a direct fast link to the emotional centre of the brain, especially if the music is associated with events in the past which evoked powerful feelings. Listening to that music immediately recreates the same emotions felt when that memory was recorded.

So why not make yourself some personal compilations of music that will, for example, bring back positive feelings to help you deal with today's challenges? Here are five different ideas for compilations that I'd find useful during difficult times:

- **For excitement (especially with just life itself)** – Scott Joplin ragtime music, because it recreates the memory of my first baby daughter dancing delightedly in her baby bouncer.

- **For care free gaiety** – Sevillana flamenco music, because it brings back the joyful memories of seeing people of all ages and abilities dancing joyously together at ferias.

- **For optimism** – Elvis Presley's "Blue Suede Shoes", because it brings back memories of secretive listening to pirate radio in my teen years, when I felt sure that a positive change in my life and the world was possible.

- **For confidence** – the march from Verdi's *Aida*, because I listened to it on the way to a very successful talk I gave for a big, daunting audience.

- **For calm contentment** – the adagietto of Mahler's 5th symphony, because it reminds me of the treasured companionship of my husband who also loves this music.

Once you have made your own personal compilations, keep them handy, so that you can use them to change your feeling state whenever you need to.

STIMULATE YOUR CREATIVITY WITH AN ARTISTIC CHALLENGE

....

"The creative writing is going well. I am trying to work on a story about a boy whose grandfather gives him a recipe that turns mean people purple! I do find it very difficult to read my work out in a group though; it's very hard to share what I write. I am in two writing groups – one group I attend once a month and I really like the tutor and this group. We go out to the pub after the session and that's wonderful; everyone is very supportive and good fun."

....

Annette, fifty-one-year-old mother of a daughter with very serious health problems which frequently escalate into life-threatening crises

This is a recent email from Annette who originally came to see me because she needed training in confidence and assertiveness skills in order to be able to fight her daughter's battles with the health and social services. She had also started to have panic attacks and became fearful of going out, especially to places where she had to interact with people.

She learnt to manage her panic attacks and became one of the most competent people I ever met at managing to get the best out of the health and social services. But where she became stuck was when it came to looking for ways for her own needs to be fulfilled within her restricted lifestyle.

During our conversations it emerged that as a young girl Annette had a talent for creative writing. But her dream of being a writer had all her adult life been side- lined by her need to earn a living and bring up her family. We decided that a feasible activity for her would be to join a creative writing group. As the email indicates, this has proved to be very rewarding for her. The latest news is that her story did find an end and a publisher!

To stimulate her spontaneity and creativity, Annette has also now become involved with another group called the Red Hat Society. These are groups for women in middle age and beyond who meet all around the world. Their aim is to encourage social interaction, fun, silliness, creativity and friendship. Members must wear red hats and purple attire to all functions.

Difficult times often demand creative thinking. This is because past ways of doing and achieving may no longer be possible or appropriate. Ironically, when you are under severe stress your lateral thinking "muscles" can virtually seize up. You need to be relaxed before new ideas can spring into your mind. How many great ideas arrive un-invited as you are out walking the dog or lying in the bath or half asleep in bed?

But rather than wait for this to happen, you can nudge this kind of thinking into action by doing anything that stimulates your spontaneity and creativity. Many artists use "warm-ups" before they get down to serious work. In drama and dramatherapy sessions we play fun games that demand spontaneous responses. The artist will often just doodle or paint what comes into his or her head before starting back to serious work on a painting. Writers who have been hit by one of those famous "blocks" usually stop for a break. Many of those I know also dabble in at least one other creative activity. So they will do something like improvising on the piano, dancing to jazz, "playing" with paints, doodling or even going into the kitchen and concocting a new kind of meal out of whatever ingredients happen to be around.

So go ahead and be spontaneous. And if, as in the case of Annette, your artistic challenge is one that you have always wanted to try or were good at in your childhood, your morale boost will be even greater.

"WHEN I WAS FORTY, MY HUSBAND LEFT ME UNCEREMONIOUSLY. I FELT HE HAD JUST WALKED OVER A DOORMAT. HE SUGGESTED I GOT A SECRETARIAL JOB. INSTEAD I BOUGHT A CAMERA."

Fay Godwin, photographer

2:3

CREATE A
SAFE HAVEN

When our world is in tumult, it is only natural to want to barricade ourselves away and wait for the storm to pass. Though hiding from the outside world is not a solution, having a calm and serene place to retreat to and feel safe and secure to experience our feelings to the fullest can be a wonderful help. The exercises in this section will help you identify and build your own haven, whether that is at home, work or somewhere else entirely.

CLEAR THE CLUTTER

Whose home couldn't do without having at least some clutter cleared out?

Some years ago we moved house to much smaller accommodation. We must have halved our possessions at that time, but we still clung on to a lot and filled a large storeroom with it. To this day, we haven't even discussed entering this room. And, I am now finding it hard to even recall what is in there that we thought was too important to lose!

Clearing your home of accumulated clutter is a simple energising task that never fails to leave you with a self-satisfied smile. It is also one that inevitably stimulates envy and elicits admiring comments from friends and neighbours. Because it has such self-esteem-boosting and motivational powers, I often suggest it as therapeutic "homework" for clients. It is particularly good as a constructive interim task when you are feeling depowered by the "big" difficulties or when you have to wait for something to be resolved or clarified before you can move on. It also works well as a healing "closure" ritual when you want to say "goodbye" to a relationship, job or home.

Here are a few tips to help you clear some clutter:

- Take three rubbish bags or boxes and label them: "Charity", "Recycling" and "Rubbish".

- Set a date and time for completing your task. This could be the same day or it could be a week or month later so that you complete the task over some weeks. But whatever the time frame you choose, start with one major sorting session as soon as you can.

- Try to stay guided by your first impulse to let go of something. It is almost always right.

- Let a friend know when you have finished and if possible celebrate together. If you are using it as part of your emotional healing after a hurt, a ceremonial ripping, burial or burning of a few "significant" items can work wonders. You will find yourself itching to move on to the next chapter of your life.

KNOW WHAT TO
SNIFF AND SMELL

*"You may break, you may
shatter the vase, if you will,
But the scent of roses will hang
around still."*

Thomas More, Renaissance scholar
and statesman

I love this quote – the reminder that even when life (the
vase) has been shattered, the memories and good feelings
of its beautiful moments (the roses) will remain and can
still be evoked.

We can also add scientific understanding to the wisdom
behind Thomas More's philosophising. We now know
that the response centre for smell is located in the most
primitive region of the emotional brain where memories are
stored. This is why scents evoke an instant feeling response
and will, more often than not, evoke memories as well.

When I return home from a spell in our house in Spain, I often find it hard to settle back in to my London life, especially on a dark, gloomy day. Once, when I was feeling stressed at the thought of a few weeks of being chained to my computer, I decided to go out and buy some jasmine oil. Burning this immediately uplifted my mood; it recreated the pleasurable, relaxed sensation that I feel when the scent of the jasmine wafts through our Spanish home.

Try using this primitive mechanism whenever you need an emotional lift. Choose a scent that you associate with happier times. If there isn't oil to burn or a scent to spray, use your imagination. By recalling your memory and concentrating on recreating the aromas in your mind, you make your body produce the good feelings associated with those memories. Now practise recreating the pleasurable sensations evoked by these scents:

- **Fresh-cut summer grass**

- **Sea air**

- **A bowl of fresh rose petals**

- **Your favourite scent**

- **Your favourite meal**

2:4

BOOST YOUR
BRAIN

Difficult times can have a major negative effect on the brain. Your mind can feel "fuzzy", so that you feel you just cannot "think straight"; it can be filled with ideas or worries that whirl around relentlessly at an exhausting speed; or, of course, it can just "go blank" at the very moment you need it most. A major trauma and prolonged stress can also have a detrimental effect on memory and the ability to concentrate.

A number of the tips in this section will help you to gain firmer control of your mind and keep it working in optimum power mode. This is so important when you are going through changes and often need your mind to feel sharper, so that you can think more quickly, as well as more laterally. There are also tips which will help you to "feed" it literally, in nutritional terms, and also to stimulate its neural activity to enable you to think more positively and flexibly. And there are ideas which will help you to ensure that it has top-quality rest, even if your sleep is disturbed, as so often is the case at difficult moments in life.

USE "SCRAP" TIME TO STRETCH YOUR MENTAL MUSCLES

· ·

"I tried to think of it as a journey of self-exploration."

· · · · · · · · · · · ·

Terry Waite, British hostage
held in Beirut

I hope none of you reading this have had such a testing challenge as Terry Waite's, but many other ongoing problem situations can require that you "sit it out" for a period of time:

- After a bereavement, it can take many months until the will is finally sorted.

- An illness may require that you "do nothing" for a time, while tests are done or various treatments are tried; or you may need an extended period of convalescence.

- In a credit crisis, you are usually advised to "sit tight" until the financial winds blow more favourably.

- After a separation or a divorce it can take a long time for financial and access matters to be sorted.

- Parents of difficult teenagers are told to be patient and just "be there" until they "grow out of it", so they put their own plans on hold.

- After a redundancy, there may be long periods of waiting for the right job to come up and not being able to make many plans so that you can be ready and available in case you are called for an interview.

- If you are involved in a legal process, you may not be given much notice of when your presence will be quickly required.

- If you are living in a warzone you may not be able to move on in the way you would like to until peace returns.

These are times when a sense of personal powerlessness can creep in. There is then a real risk of slipping into depression or going into a kind of apathetic or even a zombie-style mental state. This is especially so if the crisis has been a big one and has required a great deal of "fire-fighting" action.

One way of ensuring that you remain positive and your mind stays sharp is to view this period as a great opportunity for personal learning and development.

On the following pages are some examples of what has helped others to do this. Bear in mind that you will reap the most benefit if you choose to do something that you are not already good at and that also has some pleasurable motivating appeal for you.

WAYS TO USE SCRAP TIME TO STRETCH YOUR BRAIN'S MENTAL AGILITY

- Buy or borrow a Brain Trainer (a hand-held electronic "toy" designed to stimulate your thinking and memory powers through word and number "games", usually created in conjunction with neuroscientists). My husband's short-term memory improved demonstrably after my daughter gave him one of these for Christmas.

- Become a puzzle freak. All manner of puzzles can be picked up very cheaply in second-hand or charity shops. Or just ask your neighbours if they have any they are not using. These could be a jigsaw, crossword, Sudoku, Rubiks cube, word search or anything else that you don't usually do.

- Go to a pub, church or company quiz night or, better still, offer to join the team!

- Learn a new language and give yourself real-life opportunities to practise.

- Invent stories for your children instead of just reading to them.

- Read self-help books... and try to do what they recommend!

- Do a short cookery course and improvise with recipes.

- Do an Open University short course which requires you to think for yourself and not just acquire information.

- Learn a new computer programme or how to use a facility you need, but thought you couldn't master. (With my next piece of scrap time I will learn how to create an Excel spread sheet!)

- Learn a skill that will be useful at home: how to put up shelves, prune roses, re-grout tiles and mend a leak are just a few on my pending list. Use your friends and neighbours as teachers and offer to do something for them in return.

QUICK FIX:
Get napping

Neuroscientists have found that a nap can boost the brain's relational memory function. While you are dozing away, your brain is doing some very important filing work. It creates conceptual connections between masses of independent details, enabling you to retrieve memories much more quickly and apply the learning from them more widely.

Another piece of research compared the positive effects of napping to a more widely used brain energiser – caffeine. Guess which came out the winner?

A nap can take place almost anywhere. Some people can do it standing up, waiting in a queue, but most find that they need to take theirs dozing in a chair or lying on a flat surface. Ten to fifteen minutes is usually the optimum time for a nap or siesta. Research has shown that after 30 minutes or longer you are likely to fall into a deeper sleep which will leave you feeling groggy, rather than refreshed.

DEAL DECISIVELY
WITH DITHERING

....

"Nothing is more difficult, or therefore more precious than the ability to decide."

....

Napoleon Bonaparte, French military
leader and emperor

Difficult times often confront us with seriously difficult decisions such as:

- Where do I live now?

- How do I earn my living now?

- Should I get a divorce or not?

- Should I train for a different career?

- Should I have this risky operation or not?

- Should I tell the police or not?

One of the knock-on effects of these pending dilemmas is that everyday choices like, "Tea or coffee?" or, "What should I wear?" begin to feel stressful. It's as though your brain's decision-making powers have just frozen up.

If this has started to happen to you, I hope it helps to know that it's normal and understandable. First of all, give yourself a break from making the minor decisions and delegate these whenever you can. Reserve your energy for the more important ones.

Next, for one important decision that you are concerned about, follow the ten-step strategy below. Doing this will help you because it stimulates the thinking centres in your brain and eases you out of the predominating emotional state which is stopping you from thinking clearly.

TEN STEPS TO MAKING A GOOD DECISION

1. Set a date/time for your decision day or hour.

2. Gather information – consult research; write down facts; consult others with information, experience and opinions to share.

3. Make a "Decision Factors List", highlighting the key elements that have a bearing on your choice. It is important to select factors that are relevant to your particular decision. The number of categories you have will depend on the complexity of the decision.

In the example that follows, the person has highlighted six key aspects with regard to choosing a career and put them in priority order, where six is the most important.

DECISION FACTOR	PRIORITY ORDER
Minimises financial pressure	4
Easier to implement	1
Involves a low level of risk	3
Motivational for me	6
Minimal disruption for my family	5
Morally OK for me	2

4. Next, draw a grid like **Grid A** on p.130–31, listing your choices on the left-hand column, with the decision factors in the columns on the right. Rate your decision factors on a scale of one to three, where one is the least likelihood of achieving them.

5. Now give yourself a break – try to do something absorbing that takes your mind off the subject and, preferably, relaxes you. If possible, sleep on it for one night.

6. Review what you have written and, if necessary, make changes to your scores. Then, once you are happy with the scores, multiply all your ratings of three by the rank order number you allocated in your original decision-factor list. Then add all the scores for each choice together. So the new grid would look like **Grid B** on p.132–33.

7. Your total column should reveal the "winner" – i.e. the one with the highest mark. If it's a "draw", repeat the exercise with those factors that scored two and this will provide a result. However, bear in mind in such circumstances that there may be very little to choose between the options, so you may need to give further serious thought to the pros and cons related, I would suggest, to the most important decision factors.

8. Write down your final decision – most people have more commitment to written resolutions.

9. Share it with certain people; these should be people who can commit to asking you at a certain time later whether you implemented your decision.

10. Act as quickly as you can to implement your decision. At the very least, take one action almost immediately that will kick off the process. This will help seal your commitment and give you a great morale boost at the same time.

"THE WORST THING YOU CAN DO IS TO WAIT UNTIL A DECISION IS FORCED ON YOU — OR MADE FOR YOU."

John S. Hammond, author and expert in decision-making and former professor of the Harvard Business School

Decision grids

Grid A

CHOICES	DECISION FACTORS		
	Minimises financial pressure	Easier to implement	Low risk
A: Stay in boring job – poor prospects/salary	2	3	2
B: Pursue new job offer – better prospects/ salary (involves moving)	3	2	3
C: Leave job to become self employed	1	1	1

DECISION FACTORS

Motivational for me	Minimal disruption for family	Morally OK for me
1	3	1
3	2	3
2	1	2

Grid B

CHOICES	DECISION FACTORS		
	Minimises financial pressure	Easier to implement	Low risk
A: Stay in boring job – poor prospects/salary	2	3x1=3	2
B: Pursue new job offer – better prospects/salary (involves moving)	3x4=12	2	3x3=9
C: Leave job to become self employed	1	1	1

Motivational for me	Minimal disruption for family	Morally OK for me	Total
1	3x5=15	1	18
3x6=18	2	3	45
2	1	2	0

QUICK FIX:
Debate with the enemy

***I have never in my life learned anything
from any man who agreed with me.***

Dudley Field Malone, civil rights lawyer

Log on to a website which has opposite views to your
own. For example, this could be the site of a newspaper
that you wouldn't normally choose to read, or a group
campaigning for a change in the law that you do not
want or a fan club of music you don't like.

Open one of their chat pages and respond to some of
the comments. But don't just have a rant; respond with
a reasoned counter-argument. This should activate
your brain cells!

UNCOVER THE POSSIBILITIES FOR PROGRESS

· ·

"Discontent is the first necessity of progress."

· · · · · · · · · · ·

Thomas A. Edison, scientist
and inventor

The great American inventor Thomas Edison's own life story is a great example of this piece of wisdom in action. It also demonstrates how you can learn its lesson the hard way by living through tough times.

Thomas, the last of seven children, experienced his first serious period of discontent in early infancy. He didn't learn to talk until he was four years old which, for a child with such an enquiring and demanding mind, must have been torture. Thomas was later asked to leave his school because the teachers were so aggravated by his behaviour and lack of progress; his mind continually wandered from the task he was given. With the knowledge we now have about learning problems, we can guess that he had some kind of attention deficit disorder. We could also make a good guess that his problems had a lot to do with being a gifted child in a school environment which could not hope to satisfy his quick-thinking and creative mind.

As if the set-up of Thomas's brain didn't already bring him more than his fair share of discontent, he also suffered from a hearing disability. This appears to have started in childhood and become progressively worse in adulthood. No doubt his frustrations with this particular difficulty had some bearing on his interest in developing one of his later inventions – the phonograph.

In his early teen years, on his own initiative, he started to sell sweets and newspapers on trains as a way of supplementing his income. Again, something positive was to emerge from this enforced need to make money – he would become one of the greatest entrepreneurial businessmen of his era.

However, it was his developed character trait of positive persistence in the face of seemingly impossible odds that helped him most to become a man who is commonly considered to be the father of the electrical and technological revolution that would change the world so dramatically. When he first encountered the earliest light bulb, fifty years of effort had already been spent on trying to make this remarkable invention become commercially viable.

So when you find yourself struggling to believe that anything positive can emerge from the frustration of challenge after challenge, remind yourself of Edison's story and another of his famous quotes:

"I HAVE NOT FAILED. I'VE JUST FOUND TEN THOUSAND WAYS THAT WON'T WORK."

Thomas Edison, scientist and inventor

2:5

MAKING CONNECTIONS

Our families, friends and colleagues are so often our first port of call when we need comfort in times of crisis and without a strong network life can feel very lonely. The exercises in this section will help you to look at your social network and identify its strengths and, perhaps, weaknesses. They will also give you the tools needed to make new connections, strengthening your circle of support in the process.

CURE BOUTS OF DESPAIR WITH HUMOUR

However hard you may try to keep thinking positively, bouts of despair are likely to kick in from time to time.

Sometimes, if you catch them early, humour can help to snap you out of them. Laughter releases tension, and laughing together with a group of people can bring you closer so that you become more mutually supportive.

In the weeks following my nineteen-year-old daughter's death, I was frequently at the point of total despair. One afternoon, I was in such a state when a group of Laura's close friends and her boyfriend came round to see me. Like my daughter, they too were in their late teens. None of them had ever had to face a loss and shock such as this. Not only had they lost someone who they loved and had been, in their words, "the leading light" of their group, they also had to face the fragility of life, even for people of their young age. Because they were in this emotionally turbulent state and still very young, they acted very spontaneously, with very little concern about what was the wrong or right way to behave in this situation. They cried and hugged me, as well as each other, but then they sat down and began recalling lots of fun times with Laura and, in particular, funny things she had done and said. We found ourselves roaring with laughter as each person (including me) shared their humorous anecdotes.

If someone had told me before this happened that I might take part in such a "session" so soon after the death of one of my daughters, I would have forcibly assured them that this would not be possible. I had to live through this experience to believe it could happen and also to accept that, even in this stage of raw grief, laughter about a deceased loved one has the power to heal and positively bond people together.

Psychologists specialising in research into this subject report that joking appears to be a genuine psychological need in the face of bad situations, and is common even in major disasters and horrific war situations. Prisoners of war in Vietnam who were in solitary confinement found they could tap out jokes to each other through their walls. Hostages like Brian Keenan and John McCarthy have both said that the sense of humour that they shared helped them to bond together in spite of differences in their backgrounds and personalities. Psychologists have suggested that as well as being a stress reliever, humour can help because it gives you a sense of power.

If your problems are in any way due to illness or infirmity, laughter is especially important, as it stimulates the flow of oxygen around your body. Laughing regularly produces more endorphins and encephalin, which lift your mood and suppress pain. Laughter also produces a protein called immunoglobin which is known to kill germs and promote the white blood cells which fight off infection. The more intense and regular the laugh, the more oxygen flows around your body and the more toxic carbon dioxide is released.

So although you may not feel like doing so, make a special effort to ensure that you experience more of the things which are likely to trip you into a humorous mood such as:

- **watching comedies**

- **having fun nights out with humorous friends (laughter is infectious)**

- **dipping into books of cartoons or humorous quotations.**

QUICK FIX:
Shun the grumpy but not the occasional grumble

A good grumble to a friend or acquaintance is a great way to express your feelings. But make sure that it is to the kind of friend who is essentially a positive person and one who will comfort you. Avoid full-time moaners who are guaranteed to make you feel even worse because they are compelled to top your story with a stream of even greater problems of their own.

FILL IN THE SUPPORTIVE FRIENDSHIP GAPS

....

"If a man does not make new acquaintances as he advances through life, he will soon find himself alone. A man should keep his friendships in constant repair."

....
Samuel Johnson, author

You may think that you don't have the time or energy to go out seeking new friends right now. But identifying the gaps in your friendship network and filling them with new, supportive people can be wonderfully affirming.

However, it will also help you greatly if you develop new friendships in a steady, step-by-step way. Of course, there will be exceptions, as there are to every rule, and occasionally we seem to "click" straight into a deep relationship at step one. Generally though, it is wise to play friendship-building safely and slowly, especially when you are in a stressed and, therefore, a possibly vulnerable state.

Use the following steps as a guide, only moving on from one to the next if the last one has gone well. If it hasn't, it is unlikely that this is the kind of person you need as a friend right now, and it's easier to extract yourself at an early stage of a relationship than to wait until expectations, habits and emotional connections have been firmly established.

Step 1

Increase your opportunities to make very general safe "small talk" to become more familiar with each other.

Step 2

Encourage topics of conversation and questions which you think will reveal the person's attitudes, beliefs and aptitudes, especially to problem situations.

Step 3

Suggest ways to strengthen your connection with each other by doing something that feeds an interest or need you both share. This could be, for example, going to see a film or watch a match together. Or, if you are from different countries, but both have an interest in food and cooking, you could suggest that you each prepare a meal that is typical of your cultures.

Step 4

Start to be more self-revealing. (Note that this step comes before you start to ask them personal questions.) Share something about your likes and dislikes, hopes and dreams.

Step 5

If they show willingness to share, encourage them to talk more revealingly about their plans and hopes and problems in relation to achieving these. But always be sensitive to any signs of reluctance. You can have a great friendship with someone even though you are not equally self- revealing. A much more important key to friendship success is that each person feels that their needs and personality is respected by the other.

Step 6

Try to find a way to help them. This could be by giving them a useful contact, or by passing on some information from a website you found, for example. Alternatively, you could offer to do something practical for them. Make it clear that your help comes with no strings attached.

Step 7

Share more about your own difficult situation that might reveal your needs. If all is going well with the development of your relationship, your new friend will almost certainly offer to help in some way; and when they do, you should accept it, whatever it is. A mutual exchange of help is one of the greatest ways to move a relationship forward.

If your new friend can't help you right now, they should let you know that they are sorry about not being able to support you. And they should indicate that there is a good reason why this is so at the moment. For your friendship to progress, you don't need to have immediate help from them. Nor do you need to know why they can't currently offer support, but you do need to feel that they would be there to support you either emotionally or practically if they could be.

Step 8

The next time your friend offers help or you want to ask them for support, try to ensure that you receive the kind that fits with your needs (i.e. the current gaps in your supportive friendship). If their offer isn't a good match and you think they could offer some other kind of help, say something like this: "Actually, I already have a couple of people who babysit, but I know you used to work in a bank. I wouldn't mind a bit of advice about..."

"THERE ISN'T MUCH THAT I CAN DO, BUT I CAN SHARE AN HOUR WITH YOU, AND I CAN SHARE A JOKE WITH YOU . . . AS ON OUR WAY WE GO."

Maude V. Preston, writer

WHERE CAN YOU FIND NEW SUPPORTIVE FRIENDS?

In the main there are three kinds of opportunities to extend your social network:

- You can get to know some of your existing acquaintances better, seeking out those, for example, whom you know have also been through a tough time and appear to have come through it well.

- You could be more proactive about starting up conversations with "likely suspects" who you come across on your course through life. Always be on the lookout for interesting bits of information and news that will provide safe small-talk openers. If, for example, you travel a good deal on trains, you could prepare some talking points by doing an Internet search for interesting comparative statistics on rail travel in different regions or countries. This kind of information would have the added bonus of lifting everyone's spirits should you be on an overcrowded train or caught in a hold-up together. Always take care not to probe with questions on sensitive subjects, such as religion, politics or family. And it should go without saying that personal comments are a big no–no as conversation-openers.

- Ask your existing friends and contacts to introduce you to any of their friends or contacts who fit with the qualities you are looking for. A good example is that of Gill, a single mother, whose son, Rob, was being charged with possession of a drug. Gill knew that a cousin of one of her friends was a drug counsellor. She managed to arrange to get herself invited to the pub where the drug-counselling team socialised after work, and there she began a friendship with a woman who was very supportive when Rob's case came to court.

INVEST MORE TIME IN YOUR COMMUNITY

* *

"The best portion of a good man's life – his little nameless acts of kindness, unremembered acts of kindness."

. . . .

William Wordsworth, poet

One of the comments people most commonly make after a major disaster has hit a community is how it brought people together to help and comfort each other. More often than not, when I talk to people who are going through a private hell and ask them if there is anyone nearby to whom they can turn for support, they cannot think of anyone they know well enough to ask. Admittedly, I do most of my work in London, but I understand that this phenomenon is not exclusive to large, metropolitan areas.

I have moved house too many times in my life to be able to keep count. As a result, I have become something of an expert at finding ways to become quickly integrated into communities. Offering to volunteer to help with or initiate a community project has been, for me, one of the quickest and most satisfying ways in.

In my experience, it pays to think and plan before rushing in to help with the first project you encounter or are requested to help with. In order to obtain the best return in terms of helping the community, while at the same time boosting your own morale, you will need to bear several things in mind.

Research and respect local needs

You can do this by asking neighbours and meeting leaders of local organisations. It also helps to spend time reading the local newspaper and listening to any local radio station. You may have to put your passionate desire to be part of a book group on the back burner if all anyone else wants to talk about at the moment is how to prevent building work on their green belt.

Try to match a local need or interest to one of your talents

If you are a good organiser, you could offer to put on trips for the residents' association, or be on the committee of a charity or pressure group. If your talent is writing, you could perhaps, offer to start a newsletter. If you have years of driving experience, you could join the pool of car drivers for the local hospice. Playing to your strengths will be much more satisfying for you and make your involvement much more effective.

Under- rather than over-commit

This is much easier said than done (over-commitment is one of my weaknesses!). Every community and charitable project is run on shoestrings and is constantly thirsty for help. It is particularly hard to say no in crises, but remember – these are inevitable and frequent in this world. So you have to be clear about the commitment you can give, and stick within your capability boundaries with super- assertiveness. Remind yourself that over-commitment leads to resentfulness, bitterness and burnout – none of which will endear you to others or build your morale.

QUICK FIX:
Strengthen your colleague support

"It is an absolute bonus to make friends out of colleagues."

Jennifer Aniston, actress

Share as much of your load as you can with trustworthy colleagues. If it is not appropriate to give details of your problem, simply say something like: "It is personal, but I'm having a tough time at the moment." By sharing in this way, you will almost always receive extra support.

When you let colleagues know that you are having difficulties, try also, if possible, to give them something useful to do to help. For example, suggest that having the occasional drink or lunch together to talk about subjects other than your problems will help you. This will strengthen the friendship side of your relationship and make it more likely that they will support you in other ways should the need arise.

NETWORK BEFORE YOU NEED TO DO SO

Hundreds of surveys have been carried out to identify how people find jobs, and the story is always the same. In major surveys, between 43 and 89 per cent of job-seekers said that they secured their roles through networking. There is also evidence to suggest that when a job is found this way, the job-holder is more likely to fit better into the organisational culture, have a shorter learning curve, perform to a higher degree and stay in the job longer than someone who enters the company via another route.

"No, I don't do networking. I have always hated it. I'm just not that kind of person. I wouldn't know where to start, and I'm really bad at that sort of thing. Small talk is not my scene. I'm the kind of person who is always stuck in a corner with some sad person if ever I am at a social event."

This is what John, a fifty-four-year-old executive who had just been made redundant, said at his exit interview. And his attitude is far from unusual. My husband, who works in the career-transition business, hears this kind of reaction frequently when he suggests that networking would help. And I hear similar reactions when I am helping people to move on from personal setbacks; my clients may need to network socially to find a new partner after a divorce or bereavement or need to find new friends because they have had to move home or they have fallen out irreparably with their best friend.

Many people think they are simply too busy to network and that they cannot justify putting it on their priority list until they are in desperate need of more contacts. But very often, the real reason is that they, like John, dread the thought of doing it. This may be especially true in the UK because we are a shy culture, but I have also heard many people admit to the same problem in southern Spain, where on the surface everyone appears to be much more socially confident and outgoing.

A good network, whether it is for your business or social life, should be an interactive web of people who are mutually trusting and also have a commitment to be mutually helpful. Building up such a network is a long-term project. If you move in too quickly and try to use an already established network for help before you have proved yourself to be trustworthy and helpful, you may meet a few "cold shoulders". And that is one of the most common reasons why people become disillusioned with networking.

Another reason why people give up on networking is that they don't enjoy it. When you explore the reasons for this, it almost always boils down to a lack of confidence in managing the social scene. Like John, they often say a networking event was "a waste of time" or "boring" because they always get "stuck" with certain people. This, along with so many social-skill difficulties, can easily be put right.

Once you have learnt and practised the tricks of the networking trade, anyone can do it. You don't have to be a certain personality type. Introverts and extroverts may have different styles but they can be equally successful. The skills you need for networking socially or for work are more or less the same. Here is a plan for getting you into immediate networking action:

1. **Put networking on your to-do list.**

2. **Review the networks you have already and choose three relationships to nurture more deeply right now.**

3. **Make an action plan for doing the above.**

4. Set a goal for making at least one new contact a month. This could be through joining an established network or just striking up conversations with people you don't know at work, at the school gate or in the gym. I suggest that you aim to have had a follow-up meeting or a chat on the phone or over a coffee with each person within a month.

5. Buy or borrow a book on networking for tips and advice or book yourself in for a workshop.

6. If you know a great networker, offer to buy them lunch in exchange for giving you some advice. Their wisdom could save you loads of time and disappointments.

7. Make a pledge to ensure that for the time being, when networking, you are not going to be seeking help. Your focus will be simply on getting to know other people and letting them get to know you.

8. Make another pledge to find a way to help someone in your network at least once every two weeks. This could be offering advice or passing on a contact.

9. Buy a very small book in which you can record your networking activities and new contacts and take it around with you wherever you go. Alternatively, if you use computers or a mobile phone for making notes, create a file called "Networking" immediately!

10. Check that you are enjoying your networking. If you are not, you will not be successful. If you are finding it hard-going, it is highly likely that you are not doing something right. You may need to adjust your action planning and target areas. You may need to brush up on some skills. Or, perhaps you need to change your style and network in a way that is more suited to your personality or your specific needs. For example you may find one-to-one encounters much more enjoyable and satisfactory than party gatherings (or vice versa).

For more help, check out a book written by my husband, Stuart Lindenfield (who runs masterclasses in networking), and myself – a self-help guide which addresses most common difficulties in this area: *Confident Networking for Career Success and Satisfaction.*

2:6

STAND UP
AND OWN UP

Throughout this book we have examined how people tend to sabotage their own recovery. We have acknowledged, for example, that many of us do this by not taking good enough care of our stressed bodies and minds, by letting ourselves sink into negative thinking or by holding back when it comes to asking for the support we need. But there are, of course, many different ways in which others can sabotage your recovery process, and the tips in this section focus on preventing this from happening.

The tips in this section will help you to be self-protective without getting into de-energising fights. Taking assertive action will definitely improve your self-confidence and morale and could improve your relationship with your saboteurs as well. This is particularly true if someone has been trying to help you, but has been doing so in a way that is wrong for you.

REMIND YOURSELF OF YOUR PERSONAL RIGHTS

. . . .

It is amazing to me how, in very difficult problem situations, even truly nice people can become critical, arrogant, know-alls and interfering busy-bodies. Often, their intentions are very well meaning, but their interference and dogmatic advice are not helpful. This could be because you are not ready to take the action they suggest, or you want to try doing it in your own way, even if it might not work out right.

I admit that I too can become one of those people, when someone I care about deeply is in distress. My horrible, bossy side takes over from my nurturing one. Luckily, my family are assertive enough to tell me to back off, but less confident friends will unfortunately tend to just go quiet on me. With a few sad exceptions, I can now spot this happening. But this wasn't always the case. Before going through many years of personal and professional development training, I didn't have enough self-awareness and sensitivity to spot emotional clues from others to stop this sabotaging behaviour from damaging relationships.

Perhaps you have already encountered this kind of annoying hindrance from others. If so, I hope you have managed to give them the "back-off" message. But if you find that difficult to do, you may first need to firm up your belief in your rights to do this.

The exercise below will help you to fix your personal rights in your memory, after which you should find that when you encounter sabotaging behaviour, one or more of these rights will instantly spring into your mind. Some people say that it is like having a guardian angel (or me!) sitting on their shoulder, reminding them to stand up for themselves.

SMOKE THE VIPERS OUT OF THE NEST

· ·

If someone is trying to rile you, use the simple assertiveness technique of "fogging" to tip them off your back; this is a brilliant tactic for dealing with people who are intent on picking a fight. They back off instantly because it creates a kind of verbal smokescreen between you (hence its name) and gives them the impression (though *not* correctly) that you have given in. It is far less stressful than giving them the fight they want.

Here's an example:

The viper: "You brought this on yourself, you know. You married her. I told you she was no good for you."

Your fogging response: "You could be right. Perhaps I shouldn't have married her."

The use of the words "could" and "perhaps" is where the

smokescreen comes in. Swallow your wounded pride (you can always reboot your self-esteem later if you need to). Just enjoy the satisfaction of seeing the viper lost for words! If you don't believe it works, practise it with a friend first.

POLITELY PUSH BACK PUT-DOWNERS

"We are injured and hurt emotionally, not so much by other people or what they say, but by our own attitude and our own response."

Maxwell Maltz, self-help guru
and author

Put-downs are a type of remark or behaviour that directly or indirectly disrespects one of your personal rights. They can sabotage you by deflating your self-confidence and motivation. Sometimes they are very hard to spot at the time they are given. But afterwards, you can feel a bit uncomfortable and irritated, even though the person appeared to be being nice.

1. **Learn to quickly recognise and label put-down behaviour. The list of examples below will help.**

2. Remind yourself of your appropriate right.

3. Give an assertive response without unnecessarily justifying your case or becoming overly defensive. It is a waste of positive energy to debate with a put-downer. But beware – they are good at provoking an argumentative response.

If you do not realise you have been put down until later, don't let your feelings fester and do nothing. Write down what was said and then compose an appropriate response. Practise saying your response out loud. You could talk through possibilities with an assertive friend and rehearse using role-play with them. Next time you will be sure to respond assertively.

Here are some common styles of put-downs and suggestions for an assertive response.

Prying

Example
"I know you don't want to talk about what happened, but can you just give me an idea of who was involved?"

Your right
You have the right to privacy.

Assertive response
"What happened is still something I want to keep private."

Nagging

Example
"Isn't it time you started looking for a new girlfriend?"

Your right
You have a right to move on at your own pace.

Assertive response
"When the time is the right, I'll get another girlfriend."

Lecturing

Example

"You shouldn't just take the first job that is offered. You should take more account of the long-term prospects."

Your right

You have the right to make your own decisions and cope with the consequences.

Assertive response

"I want to take this job. It could turn out to be the wrong choice, but if that happens, I'll deal with it."

Questioning your choice

Example

"Are you sure you are making a wise choice to stay with him after he has deceived you so badly?"

Your right

You have a right to choose who you want to be with.

Assertive response

"I am making the right choice for me."

Unwanted advice

Example

"I know two people who went to see therapists and both found the experience a waste of time and money. I think you have the guts to beat this on your own."

Your right

You have a right to seek professional help if you choose.

Assertive response

"I have made the appointment and that's that."

Insulting labels

Example

"You Easterners are so deferential to your elders. You shouldn't let your father determine your life."

Your right

You have a right to be treated as an individual.

Assertive response

"I am an individual and so is my father. What other people from the East do is not relevant."

QUICK FIX:
Focus on the "why" when the "how" gets tough

Find or make a pictorial representation of the light you can see (or want to see) at the end of your tunnel. For example, this could be:

- the joining of male and female hands (to represent a new partnership)

- the garden of your new home

- the logo of a major company – your new job

- a dove sitting on a map of your country (to indicate peace).

Whenever the going appears to be getting too tough: look and digest.

DEAL HEAD-ON WITH YOUR WORST-CASE SCENARIO

· ·

"Only the unknown frightens men. But once a man has faced the unknown, that terror becomes the known."

· · · · · · · · · · · · · ·

Antoine de Saint Exupery, author

Fear is undoubtedly one kind of motivator that can spur you into action. As long as you can control your fear though, you can use it positively to help keep you going (and that's almost certainly why it exists).

Here is an exercise that involves using your imagination to bring your worst fear out of the shadows so you can deal with it head-on. You can then rehearse ways to calm your heart's emotional response and prepare a constructive contingency plan to include practical actions that you can take immediately. Doing all this will put your mind at rest and enable you then to forget this worst-case scenario and get on with living positively for today and moving on in an optimistic way to the future.

1. Create a picture of your worst-case scenario in your mind's eye. Alternatively, write your scenario out as a story. Use the present tense to bring it more to life. When you have finished it, read your story out loud as though it has just happened. You can do this on your own or with a friend. Either of these creative techniques should activate the fight/flight fear response in your body.

2. Use the breathing exercise on p.39 to calm down your pulse if it has started to race. You could also use the mindfulness technique (p.37) to visualise your heart beating and pumping through your veins to slow it down to its normal rate.

3. Now that you are physically calm, write out a contingency plan for yourself using the outline opposite to ensure that you deal with the situation effectively and recover emotionally as well.

4. Note down the action you are going to take in the *immediate* future to ensure that your worst-case scenario does not become a reality.

For example:

✓   I am going to eat and drink more healthily.

✓   I am going to network twice a week to increase my chances
    of getting a job as quickly as possible.

✓   I am going to take advice about managing my money better.

✓   I am going to disclose our family problem to one trusted
    friend for support. I am also going to seek advice from the
    substance abuse centre to see how best I can help my son.

✓   I am going to ensure that my mother does the brain
    exercises recommended by the Alzheimer's Society.

5. Note down any *immediate* action you could take to help
    others cope with the situation, if you fear you are not
    going to be around:

✓   Ring lawyer regarding revisions to my will.

✓   Ring my brother and talk through my fears and plans and
    give him the name of my lawyer.

✓   Set up a contingency savings fund.

✓   Contact the funeral directors and ask for funeral costings,
    etc. and set this money aside in a special account that my
    brother can access.

6. Give yourself a special treat which will divert your attention well away from this subject.

"THE THING YOU FEAR HAS NO POWER. YOUR FEAR OF IT IS WHAT HAS THE POWER."

Oprah Winfrey, TV presenter

OUTLINE FOR A CONTINGENCY PLAN

- Summary of feared outcome.

- Make a list of the specific impacts that this could produce in each of the following areas of your life:

  - Personal relationships and home life

  - Working life

  - Finances

  - Physical health

  - Emotional wellbeing

  - Social life

- Make a note of the names of the key people whom you could call to help and support you with these particular issues, or to support your dependants or loved ones, if you think there's a chance you will not be around. Ensure that you also have their contact details readily at hand.

- Note what action you (or others) could take to cope with this situation and deal with its effects in each of the relevant areas of your life. If you cannot think of anything you or others could do, ring a few of the support people you listed above for ideas. Trust that they will have the answers that either your fear or inexperience is stopping you from recognising.

- Test out any aspects of your plan that can be tested. For example, walk the escape route if you fear a fire or terrorist attack on a building you are in. Survivor research has shown that this kind of testing increases your chances of surviving considerably.

- File this plan somewhere safe and, if you think this is necessary, inform others in your life where it can be found.

QUICK FIX:
Get greener

Going greener can save you loads of money, as well as benefitting the planet. So why not ease your budget while easing your conscience? A guaranteed winner for your morale! Make this quick and easy to do by logging on to Friends of the Earth (friendsoftheearth. uk) – they can send you a tip a day by email or text.

SAVE FOR
SPECTACULAR
SPENDING
. . . .

In the area in Spain where we have a house, weddings tend
to be very large events. Very often 500 guests are invited,
even if families are on very low incomes, and traditionally,
no expense is spared by either the host or the guests, who
buy glamorous outfits and generous presents.

One wedding I went to in the midst of the major international financial crisis of 2009 was, however, a very
different affair. The young couple, like the majority of their
friends, were highly anxious about the very likely prospect
of losing their jobs; just a quarter of the usual number of
people was invited, although those of us selected were still
treated to a luxurious feast. At the end of the meal, I was
moved to see my young friends open a present from a large
group of their friends. It was a small china piggy bank with
their names and these words written on it: "In these times
of crisis, this is what we have saved. Congratulations!"

The bride was moved to tears and, of course, so was I (as I am once again as I write this)!

When I first drafted this book, I had in mind for this tip the creation of a special savings plan, the purpose of which would be to provide resources to give yourself a special treat, such as a weekend break. During difficult times it is harder than ever to prioritise such luxuries, even though you may know you desperately need them.

I would still suggest you create this kind of saving fund for treats, but my young friends' wedding gift was a wonderfully different example of spectacular "spending". It made me think that slowly accumulating enough money to be able to give someone a generous and unexpected gift could provide both the giver and the receiver with great morale boosts.

"YOU MAKE A LIVING BY WHAT YOU GET. YOU MAKE A LIFE BY WHAT YOU GIVE."

Winston Churchill, British Prime Minister (1940–45 and 1951–55)

DO A DEAL
WITH YOURSELF
OVER DEBT

As I said in my introduction to this book, I am writing in the midst of a global pandemic. This is already causing real financial hardship for many millions of people and is understandably triggering the rise of depression and severe anxiety over sliding into debt.

Antony Elliott, the director of FairBanking, has made a special study of how people get into debt and how they get out of it; he told me that he has absolutely no doubt that levels of morale play a significant part: "When morale is low, people tend to adopt a head-in-the-sand approach to their finances and debt. This is very concerning because we know from our research that anxiety increases in direct proportion to our debt/income ratio."

So even if you are reading this during a financial boom period, if your morale is low it could still be useful to consider ways to ensure you don't get into trouble with debt. After all, no one ever knows when their financial fortunes may change, and doing anything that will add to your overall sense of security and independence is guaranteed to give you a boost.

Here are some ideas for deals you could do with yourself right now:

- **Keep your head well out of the sand and never just sit back and hope that "something will turn up". Always respond to even a threat of financial difficulty by making some adjustment to the way you are managing or spending your money.**

- **Vow only to use cash or debit cards. Ceremoniously cut up your credit cards (or at least all but one of them, which you can keep locked away). Put the cut-up cards in a jar on your kitchen worktop at home, so you can feel smug and virtuous each time you see them! I know of one debt consultant who keeps such a jar on his desk; he insists that every new client adds theirs to his store before he will advise them.**

- **Ensure that all your regular commitments are paid by direct debit the day after your pay cheque enters your bank account. Alternatively, if you use Internet banking,** you can easily arrange for a lump sum which will cover all your bills to be sent from your current account into a savings account that does not offer a tempting debit card. It will only take you a few minutes to set this account up to make regular electronic transfers on the due dates.

- Increase your debt repayments to the highest level you can afford.

- Never borrow money from anyone just to buy a bargain. Debt advisers say that is one of the worst financial sins. (And isn't it the most tempting one too?)

- Delete all emails and/or tear up letters immediately that are offering to "buy" or "sell on" your debts. They are guaranteed to make your financial worries escalate in the not-too-distant long term. Your morale will nosedive when you realise that you have allowed yourself to be duped.

And finally, two top tips from Antony Elliot:

- Do two monthly checks: the first is on your level of expenditure, to check that it is in line with your current means; the second is on your debt/income ratio, to ensure that it is still within your means.

- Think of your money as a series of pots. Imagine that you have a finite pot of money for each of your main expenditure zones and aim to stay within your budget for each. (This is particularly helpful for young adults when they are in the early stages of learning about budgeting.)

"DEBT IS THE SLAVERY OF THE FREE."

Publilius Syrus, Roman author, first century bc

QUICK FIX:
Spend to save on an expert

If you feel you could benefit from some sound financial advice right now, you might want to consider paying for a one-off meeting with a financial adviser. It may well be worth the cost of the consultation if it helps you to make significant savings in the long term. Do take care to ensure that he or she is truly independent though, and not an insurance salesperson in disguise, as many are.

If you cannot afford to do this, think of investing some time, rather than money, in obtaining some free advice. This often entails queuing, if you go to a government or charitable agency. But there are plenty of ways you can use this waiting time productively, so it does not have to be a depressing experience. You could, for example, use the time for planning, learning something new or meditating.

A FINAL WORD

Reading through these pages you may have picked up that my own journey through life hasn't always been an easy one. My life has been peppered with all manner of setbacks and I know that there may be many more to come. It is through using the techniques described in the preceeding chapters that I have weathered my own personal storm and will continue to do so. As we reach the end of this book I hope you, too, feel prepared to batten down the hatches and see out your storm.

And you too may be aware – and fearful – of the "unknown". Perhaps you are even thinking along these lines right now, and feeling sceptical about the future, despite having read through this collection of tips. But I hope that you will soon start to put many of them into action in earnest, because when you do, you will start to feel differently. Then, in the future, should your self-confidence and trust in the world be knocked back again, you will find that the skills you have acquired for recovering your psychological power will automatically flip back into the forefront of your mind.

Most importantly, this will be true even when you cannot improve your physical or material circumstances. It was only when this happened to me personally – when my daughter Laura was killed – that I believed this could really be so. During this period, I used to repeat the following Chinese proverb to myself: "You cannot prevent the birds of **sadness** from flying over your head, but you can prevent them from nesting in your hair." I have taken the liberty of highlighting the word "sadness" here because I have found that it can be replaced with other emotions that affect morale negatively during difficult times (such as guilt, jealousy or anger), so that the proverb's wisdom can be applied in many situations.

Finally, perhaps once you are feeling stronger in yourself, you will pass on your new knowledge and insight to anyone else who may be struggling to stay positive through problem situations. Not only will this give them much needed comfort and encouragement, it will also strengthen your own morale further still.

So, good luck – and I hope that armed with the knowledge of *Weathering the Storm*, you'll find your recovery is quicker than you'd ever dreamed possible.

About Trigger Publishing

Trigger is a leading independent altruistic global publisher devoted to opening up conversations about mental health and wellbeing. We share uplifting and inspirational mental health stories, publish advice-driven books by highly qualified clinicians for those in recovery and produce wellbeing books that will help you to live your life with greater meaning and clarity.

Founder Adam Shaw, mental health advocate and philanthropist, established the company with leading psychologist Lauren Callaghan, whilst in recovery from serious mental health issues. Their aim was to publish books which provided advice and support to anyone suffering with mental illness by sharing uplifting and inspiring stories from real life survivors, combined with expert advice on practical recovery techniques.

Since then, Trigger has expanded to produce books on a wide range of topics surrounding menatnd wellness, as well as launching Upside Down, its children's list, which encourages open conversation around mental health from a young age.

We want to help you to not just survive but thrive ... one book at a time

Find out more about Trigger Publishing by visiting our website: triggerpublishing.com or join us on:

@TriggerPub
@TriggerPub
@TriggerPub

TRIGGER
he mental health & wellbeing publishe

About the Shaw Mind Foundation

A proportion of profits from the sale of all Trigger books go to their sister charity, Shaw Mind, also founded by Adam Shaw and Lauren Callaghan. The charity aims to ensure that everyone has access to mental health resources whenever they need them.

You can find out more about the work Shaw Mind do by visiting their website: shawmindfoundation.org or joining them on

@Shaw_Mind
@shawmindUK
@Shaw_Mind

the Shaw mind
FOUNDATION